Growing Strong

A book about taking care of yourself

Christina Goodings

❀

Masumi Furukawa

LION
CHILDREN'S

Contents

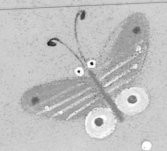

Worth the risk
Whatever the weather
Fit for anything
First aid
Dream on
To be the best

The beginning of you

Congratulations! You have been chosen for a very important job: taking care of you.

You were begun by your mother and your father. From each of them, your body was given an inner plan for how it will grow. As a result, you will look a bit like both of your parents.

Whatever you've been given, you can make sure it grows into the best it can be.

what you grow to look like depends on what your parents look like

you might be
small as a child
but still grow tall

a dog looks like
its parents too

You might look exactly
like one of your parents.
Oh well.

You can't change the person you are... but you can make the most of yourself.

Building blocks

Have you ever played with blocks? Then you will know the right kind of blocks to make a good building. Only then can you make it grow tall and strong.

Your body needs the right materials to grow. You need to eat and drink all the different kinds of things it needs. The list of these things would be very long, but there is an easy way to get them all: eat a variety of foods from the big food groups.

Remember, too, that your body is mostly water. Drink several glasses every day.

your body needs water to stay the way it should be

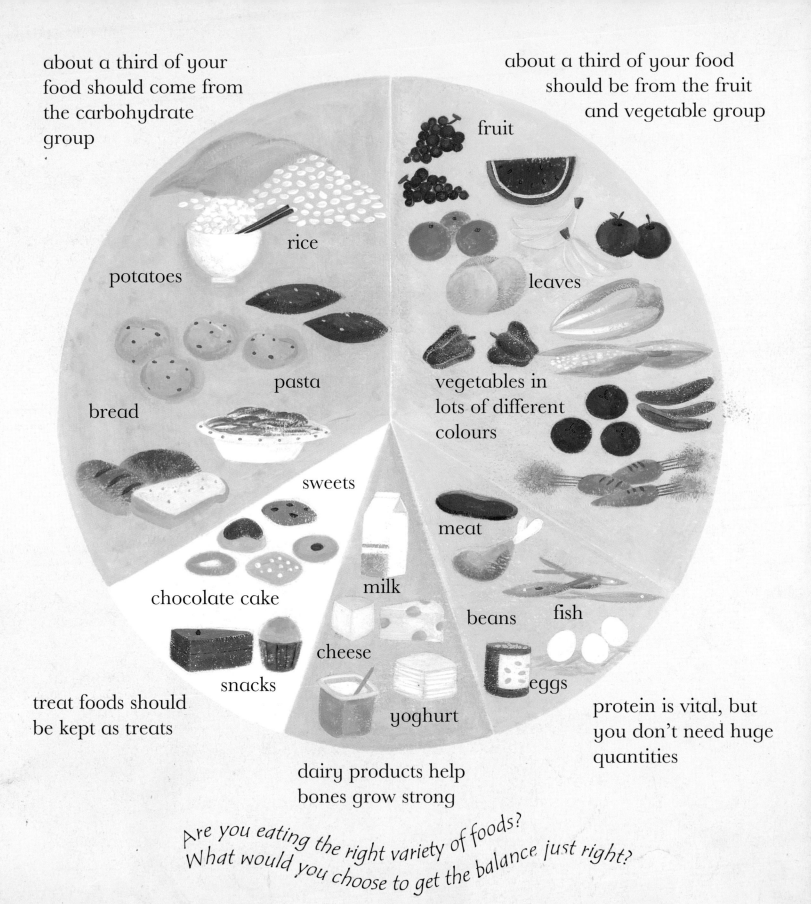

about a third of your food should come from the carbohydrate group

about a third of your food should be from the fruit and vegetable group

fruit

rice

potatoes

leaves

pasta

bread

vegetables in lots of different colours

sweets

meat

chocolate cake

milk

beans

fish

cheese

snacks

eggs

yoghurt

treat foods should be kept as treats

protein is vital, but you don't need huge quantities

dairy products help bones grow strong

Are you eating the right variety of foods? What would you choose to get the balance just right?

Fuel

A car needs fuel to power its engine. Your body needs food to power everything you do.

Even if you sit still all day, your body needs fuel energy just to keep it working. If you are active, you burn more fuel. A unit of energy is called a calorie.

running around having fun uses
up food fuel – and water too

If you eat more calories than you burn, your body stores them as fat.

Carbohydrate foods are good fuel. Treat foods have lots of calories but they can easily tempt you to eat more of them than you can burn.

after being active, your body deserves refuelling (and topping up with water)

Do you eat the right amount of fuel food for the things you do? What would the right amount be?

Keep it clean

It's a mucky world and there's no escaping it.

For one thing, your body gets rid of the mucky stuff it no longer needs – when you sweat, for example, or go to the toilet, or blow your nose. That's the first set of things to deal with.

Then there are mucky things all around. Some are obvious, such as mud. Others are unseen. Nasties that can make you ill lurk on all kinds of things from door handles to keyboards to towels.

clean hair

all-over washing

clothes get grubby and need washing too

The simplest way to deal with mucky things is to wash with soap and water. As well as making you clean, it helps you to smell nice.

wash your hands often, especially before meals and after you go to the toilet

Sometimes little creatures may choose to make their home on you. Head lice are eager to creep from one head to another. Combing your hair with a very fine comb is one way to get rid of the beasts and their eggs. Rinse the comb after each sweep.

head lice make their home in clean hair as much as dirty hair – but you can beat them

Smile

Good teeth are something to smile about. Good teeth help you munch your food. Good teeth don't hurt. Good teeth look great!

Your teeth were already in your gums when you were born. By the time you were two years old, you had your first set – of 20 teeth.

Still waiting were your grown-up teeth. These push out the baby teeth when a person is between six and eight. They are the last set of teeth that will grow… so look after them.

Be sure to brush for about three minutes twice a day. This cleans your teeth of the food leftovers where decay gets going. It also cleans the gums so they stay healthy and firm.

Clean your teeth before you go to bed each night. What is your best time for the other brushing session?

Run for your life

Your body loves being active.
 When you do activity that makes you out of breath,
your heart and lungs grow stronger.
 When you do activity that shifts your body along, your
muscles grow stronger.
                When you do activity that makes you
                bend and stretch, you get more flexible.

skip

play

Whether you are sporty or not sporty, muscle power is a great way forward!

swim

run

take advice

protect yourself
properly

The more you practise a skill, the more your body remembers how to do it right – without you even thinking!

Worth the risk

Do take care!

Some people see hazards everywhere and are scared to do anything.

Other people don't think enough about what is foolish to try.

The clever thing is to be able to spot a risk and know how to avoid it.

As you get more skilful at an activity, you can do more daring things.

decide for yourself what challenges you take on

Whatever the weather

Blazing sun, driving rain, biting wind…
  The weather out there can be wild. To stay well, you need
to protect yourself.
  The sun's rays can cause damage. Sun cream, correctly used,
can give good protection. Even so, it's better to cover up and
not stay out in the sun too long. Just getting overheated can
also make you ill.

sun shade

sunglasses

cool drink

hat for when
you're not in
the shade

use cream
to cover up
bare skin

cover-up clothing

Getting cold can make you miserable. If you get too cold, it can be dangerous because your body will shut down bit by bit. Take care when it's raining, too, because wet clothes can chill you quickly.

umbrella

a hat makes you feel cosy

waterproofs

layers of clothes trap warm air around you

boots

keep fingers and toes cosy

Choose clothes to protect your body – as well as to look good.

Fit for anything

Some people are happiest dashing about in the great outdoors.
Some people prefer other things.
Taking care of your body will help you with every kind of activity. It will even help your brain to be sharp and quick.
You should still be taking care of yourself, whatever you do.

hand work

make-and-do is fun, but
be careful with sharp tools

follow advice about how to use
equipment and materials

be kind to your ears and keep
the music to a suitable level

brain work

if you spend time at one
thing, take breaks or your
eyes, hands, and back
may suffer

Remember to practise –
and then take a break.
You'll come back fresher
and better.

art work

You can get better at whatever you love to do!

First aid

Ouch!
 It can be a hard world out there. Even if you take care and wear protective gear, things can go wrong. Not many people avoid bumps and scrapes completely – and injuries can be more serious than that.

  Happily, your body is able to repair itself in many ways. If you get injured, it's good to know what to do right away to help your body put things right.

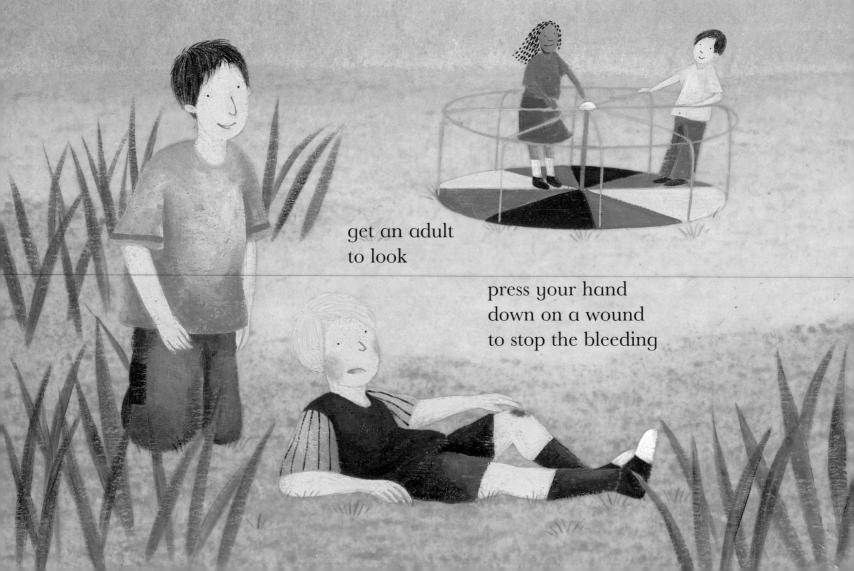

get an adult
to look

press your hand
down on a wound
to stop the bleeding

You should always check with a grown-up
to make sure everything than can be
done is done right.

don't try to move –
call for help or send
someone

to stop a bruise,
rest and apply
something cold

Help your body repair itself by taking life easy for a bit!

Dream on

Your body has so much to do: growing, dashing around, learning new things. It's no surprise that your brain and your body need plenty of sleep every day. Your body can then give more energy to growing and to repairing itself.

For example, if you have been running around a lot, your leg muscles will have suffered wear and tear. When you sleep, your body repairs them… and that's when the muscles get stronger.

Your brain, too, needs rest. It needs to dream. You sometimes remember dreams as bits and pieces of things that happened jumbled up in odd ways. In fact, your brain is simply sorting itself out and letting things go.

To sleep well, it helps to go to bed at the same time every day. It's even more important to get up at the same time every day.

uncluttered room
with things put
away neatly

the perfect sleeping place

cool and airy

truly dark once the
light is off

comfy bed

What could you do to make your sleeping place even dreamier?

To be the best

There has to be a reason for taking good care of yourself…
and there is.
To be the best you can be.
That doesn't mean that you're going to be the best
at everything. Everyone is born with different abilities.
Even so, you can make it your aim to make
the most of what you've got.

being a good friend

taking care of
the planet

As you grow up, you will also have to think about how you use your talents. What do you think is good and right and wise? What can you do to make your world a better place?

helping others

having fun

What will you do so that when you look back on your life, you will be able to say, "I was truly me"?